VIA Folios 167

Trigger

TRIGGER

Poems by Maria Famà

BORDIGHERA PRESS

Cover art by Rosario Famà, "Trigger," oil painting.

Library of Congress Control Number: 2023952519

Published by
BORDIGHERA PRESS
John D. Calandra Italian American Institute
25 W. 43rd Street, 17th Floor
New York, NY 10036

VIA Folios 167
ISBN 978-1-59954-214-0

Contents

This book is dedicated to the Generations of Writers

With infinite respect for the past

With infinite service to the present

With infinite responsibility to the future

PART ONE

THE PULL OF MEMORIES

Daddy's Little Cap

I kissed Daddy's little cap when I found it

Yes, I kissed Daddy's little cap when I found it

the little cap he wore to America in 1939

I kissed it when I found it in the cellar cedar closet in the little suitcase

he carried from Sicily   I found the little cap after my mother died

eight years after my father's death

I found it   kissed it   took it home   hung it in the cellar way closet

where I can kiss it every day

After eighty years, the little cap looks brand new

dark grey, pebbled wool, an inscription on the silk inside dome

Excelsior Prodotto Italiano Preferito

I know this little cap's story all about fitting

Daddy told me years ago

My Nonna Maria, Daddy's mother, bought the cap

for his journey to America to be with his father in New Jersey

away from Fascist Italy's grip

my father tried the cap on in the Sicilian shop

so fashionable   a perfect fit

sixteen years old, Daddy wore his new cap on the train to Palermo

he wore his new cap walking the deck that chilly March

until   until   until

his father picked him up at the New York dock

fedoras   fedoras   fedoras   everywhere fedoras

My Nonno Frank, Daddy's father, sported a movie star fedora

The friend with the auto to take them home wore a fedora

fedoras   fedoras   fedoras   on every male's head

All of a sudden, Daddy felt very poor

All of a sudden, Daddy felt he did not fit in

he was a country bumpkin in his new little cap

When they got home to the attic apartment

Nonno Frank shared with Uncle Louie, Uncle Pete, and Cousin Tony

my father saw all their fedoras hanging on hooks

he stuck his new wool cap in his little suitcase

never to be worn again

nobody in the States could wear such a hat

Nonno Frank bought my father a gray fedora

showed him how to wear it on an angle

Eighty years later, the little cap Daddy shunned

because he needed to fit in

has for me the allure and aura of a relic

I'd wear it myself if it fit but my head's too big

Every day, I kiss the little cap

Every day, I kiss the little cap

my father always in my head   always in my heart.

Women in their Kitchens

My mother Frannie said she always liked a sunny, bright kitchen

I see her in a beam of sunlight smiling over fragrant pots

on the stove and flowering pots on the windowsill

My grandmother Domenica said her tongue was always hanging out
    for greens

I see her washing and sautéing mountains of swiss chard, escarole,
    spinach, and

broccoli rabe in her fruit and flower wall papered kitchen

My grandmother Maria Concetta said there was a correct place for
    everything

in her stark, white kitchen and only one right way to do anything

I see her carefully teaching me the proper way to dry a dish

My great grandmother Mattia said she had to bake lots of biscotti

to fill the big ceramic cookie jar she kept in her blue kitchen

I see her handing me a biscotto as I sat on a red chair swinging my legs

Aunt Rosie said children needed plenty of lemonade and pastina to
    grow

I see her sitting at her kitchen table under the window cutting lemons with a huge carving knife, the pastina boiling on the range

Aunt Minne said she liked a kitchen big enough to dance in

I see her dipping and swaying to music on the radio as she cooked
    meals

to order for her husband and children in her spacious kitchen

Zia Antonia said spices were all you needed to make any dish delicious

I see her standing in her rustic, Sicilian kitchen amid hanging ropes
    of garlic bulbs,

strings of little hot red peppers, and stalks of dried oregano she'd
    grown

Cousin Toni said sometimes the Blessed Mother helped her cook
when she felt ill

I see her saying the rosary in her tidy kitchen standing at the stove

while tending a big pan of frying cutlets and a large pot of spaghetti

Cugina Maria said the Messina sea breeze wafting into the kitchen
    from the balcony

added flavor to her pasta with eggplant on hot, summer days

I see her carrying dishes onto the balcony where everyone ate under
    a canopy

Aunt Angie in New Brunswick said she needed enough food for

the constant flow of family and friends streaming through her bright
kitchen

I see her filling platters of savory meats and trays of sweet pastries

Aunt Angie on Moore Street said a clean kitchen was more important

than the elegant meals Uncle Tony, a restaurant chef, prepared

I see her scouring the sink, floor, stove, and cabinets until they
    sparkled

Aunt Nancy said Uncle Vincent's cigar smoke was an extra ingredient
in

his favorite stuffed pasta dishes she made for him in her small kitchen

I see her cooking amid the overflowing file cabinets he kept by the
table

Aunt Martha said she valued convenience and modern appliances

I see her commanding her space station galley kitchen with its

flat top electric range and spare, shiny black and silver appliances

I always say Betsy Ross would be delighted to cook in

my old fashioned kitchen   to her eyes, the old white stove

with knobs for the gas flame instead of wood for fire

the porcelain sink with hot and cold running water

would be heavenly

the refrigerator and the air conditioner miraculous

I see myself chopping, slicing, sautéing between red and blue walls

I stir in harmony with

the many essences of women in their kitchens.

Trigger

One day in late 1944

twenty-one year old Saro Famà

before he was my father

sat up in his hospital bed in

Crile Army Hospital in Cleveland, Ohio

as Roy Rogers walked into the ward

with his horse, Trigger

My soldier father   born in Sicily

Private First Class in Patton's Third Army

with battle wounds received at Metz

on the border of France and Germany

was weary yet hopeful he'd learn to walk again

he knew Roy Rogers from the movies

was thrilled to meet him and

his famous horse, Trigger

Trigger walked to each bed

hospital booties on his hooves

letting each man pet him

my father reached for Trigger who nuzzled him

a spark arose between the movie star horse

and the young immigrant warrior who drew with a quick hand

a sketch of Trigger from life right there with paper and pencil

From this sketch, Saro Famà painted in oils

a portrait of Trigger on canvas

he hung the painting in my room

when I was a little girl

I loved seeing Trigger's kind face

I loved hearing how Daddy met Trigger, petted him, drew his picture

I knew Roy Rogers and his wife Dale Evans from TV

I even had a Dale Evans wristwatch

Yet Trigger held me rapt

I've kept the painting with me through the years

It is suffused with light   compassion   nobility

Reminding me that once

my father was an ailing boy and

Trigger the celebrity

who offered him a healing touch

        of comfort

        of inspiration.

Two Sweaters

For my mother Francesca Guaetta Famà

My mother Francesca was brilliant

born twenty years later

she would have been a physician, professor, attorney

instead, she considered herself lucky

to be allowed to finish high school

    learning secretarial skills

    carrying a full academic course, too

    working during those war years

    at the Main Post Office at 30th Street

    in the wee hours of the morning

Her teachers told her she should try for a scholarship to university

Her parents told her to go to work, help the family before she married

With high school diploma in hand

Francesca went to work at Metropolitan Life Insurance Company

rising through the ranks

until she was forced to quit when she married

Met Life did not permit married women to be employees

With all her energy and insight
Francesca mothered her four children
cooked   cleaned   kept a warm, hospitable home
   always learning   always reading
   devouring her beloved medical books
she read stories and poems to us children
she took us to the library every week

Both she and my father
unable to attend university themselves
made sure all their children were educated
when I, the oldest, won a scholarship to Temple University
Francesca was thrilled that her daughter
was now a "college girl"
living at home   commuting to Temple

One summer day, before my freshman year,
my mother took me on a special trip to
Wanamaker's Department Store in Center City Philadelphia
to buy suitable clothes for her college girl
that I could mix and match
She helped me choose a jumper, two skirts, two blouses
My mother picked out for me two sweaters with buttons

one deep red   the other forest green

Francesca treated me to lunch that day at

Wanamaker's elegant, chandeliered Crystal Tea Room

we hung our handbags on the little hooks under the table

my packages of new clothes at our feet

My mother was so proud of her scholarship daughter

Scheduled to be in an Honors Program at university

I would meet people from all over the world

I was full of hope and scared

My mother's advice to me: "Just smile"

Francesca, herself, had the most dazzling smile

gorgeous   heart melting

she understood that if one smiles

people are put at ease

I loved wearing my two sweaters

they went with everything

I wore those two sweaters for years

the green sweater disintegrated from use

fifty years later, I still have the red sweater

now practically a rag

Yet, I keep it as a talisman

I keep it as a reminder of my mother's dream of

the education that she was denied and I had.

Daddy's Globe

To help us learn geography

our father bought an inflatable globe

blew up this plastic world

with his breath

green seas flowed

mountains rose

he secured the copper tubes

at the North and South Poles

onto the metal axis

placed our globe on its stand

then, Daddy spun the Earth for us

we learned to spot booted Italy

Sicily the football it kicked

our family's home

we found England, France, Germany

where Daddy fought in the War

we found the USA with its many states

Canada above   Mexico below

South America and Africa like puzzle pieces

facing each other across the Atlantic

Our father called out

China, India, Australia, Greece, Ireland, Russia

Nigeria, Ethiopia, Argentina, Brazil

we found them all in bright colors

we found the oceans, too

sometimes when Daddy was at work

we unscrewed our planet from its axis

tossed it around like a beach ball

the world containing our father's breath

in our playful hands.

My Father Built Me a House

In the video of thirty-three years ago
Aunt Nancy and I are the grown-ups
sitting with three year old Nick and one year old Mary
in the house my father built me

More than a half-century ago
in the spring when I was seven
I played in the big cardboard box
the new washer came in
I put in wooden grape boxes as table and chair
Hung up a newspaper photo of Chief Halftown
Seneca Indian local TV personality, and a
paw print autographed postcard of famous collie Lassie
that I had sent away for

When summer storms melted down the box, I cried
My father decided to design and build me
a sturdy playhouse
with love and ingenuity he built
interlocking wooden sides, a roof, carved out windows
he painted my house blue

for years, my father assembled the house when warm weather came

took it apart   stored it flat when cold winds blew

my brothers, our cousins, our chums, and I spent hours

playing games, celebrating birthdays,

dreaming ourselves grown

in the house my father built me

my father took home movies of us

jammed in the house, mugging for the camera,

toasting with cups of Hawaiian Punch

eating cake and Chunky Chocolates

in the house my father built me

Years later, my brother, Frank, set up the portable house

for his own children to play in   he painted it red

in the video he took we celebrate Aunt Nancy's 76th birthday

we talk and laugh as Nick and Mary

help her open presents

in the house my father built me

Soon, Frank will set up the house again

for his grandchildren, Emma, Michael, and Lucy to play in

I hope to sit, dream, and party with them

in the house my loving, ingenious father built for me.

Spelling Bee

The principal expected me to win
the city-wide Spelling Bee
on a Saturday In May
when I was in eighth grade

On that May day
cramps hit me hard
my body still new to them
and the flow of red

I wore my school uniform
Starched white blouse
Navy blue jumper
pinned on pads underneath

A parishioner with a big black car
picked me up and drove
to Center City Philadelphia
the stern nun principal of my school
rode in the passenger seat

Hot morning sun cooked the streets
I sat in the back seat riding a wave of nausea
nobody from my family could attend the Bee

my father was working

my mother was at home with little children and chores

For months I had been studying

lists of words to spell

  ricochet

  citation

  thesaurus

after I won bee after bee

the principal became my coach

  encyclopedia

  mendacious

  cranial

The principal expected me to win

the city-wide championship

  loquacious

  putrid

  diligent

each day after school in the principal's office

I stood in front of her dark wooden desk

she scared me as she barked out words

  officious

  dictatorial

  egotistical

the principal pointed out to me

the spot on the shelf

where she planned to place the trophy

onerous

financier

plutocracy

the principal expected me to win

non sequitur

sonnet

pompous

On that Saturday in May

I took the stage with other contestants

from various parts of the city

in a huge auditorium packed with people

the large ornate trophy stood

on the side of the stage

as I found my seat

the principal caught my eye

she pointed to the trophy

The principal expected me to win

elementary

decision

bucolic

sick   scared   exhausted

I heard in my head the word "coraggio"

my family's watchword

courage gets us through everything

with the Blessed Mother's help

it was May, her month,

I prayed for help and wondered

If the Madonna ever had such bad cramps

  muscular

  interlocutor

  formidable

Round and round we went

each contestant walked to the microphone

at center stage

the announcer called out a word

we said the word   spelled it   said it again

  insipid

  streptococcus

  torrid

the room was spinning

  chrysanthemum

  pharmacy

  frontier

the crowd was yelling and clapping

  zephyr

  miasma

  thimble

More rounds until

there were only three of us on stage

a girl   a boy   and me

spelling officials carried the tall fancy trophy

to the middle of the stage

near the microphone

   bombastic

   feasible

   exotic

round and round we went

that girl   that boy   and me

   fumble

   zeppelin

   cautious

more rounds

wet and weary   I kept praying

the principal fixed me with her eyes

pointed to the trophy

The principal expected me to win

The room tilted

   telescope

   crustacean

   lovely

the girl   the boy   and me

another ten rounds

   morbid

   applause

   dither

celebrity

aphrodisiac

notorious

sanctimonious

function

laurel

I wanted home   I wanted the trophy

I wanted the bathroom

  tentative

  wisteria

  marathon

My turn again

I rose   shaky   dizzy

to the mike

the crowd quieted

the announcer called the word

  minister

I said

"Minister, M-I-N-I-S-T-O-R, minister, Oh, NO!

It's M-I-N-I-S-T-E-R, minister."

"Sorry, you already said the word, " the announcer said

the crowd groaned

there were no do-overs

I walked off the stage
the principal grabbed me
"How could you do that!" she hissed
her eyes were on fire
she stormed out of the hall
with me and our driver rushing behind
we did not stay to see who won
Was it the boy?   Was it the girl?
Who took the big, beautiful trophy to their school?

The ride home was dark despite the sun
The principal radiated anger
She did not speak one word to me
No trophy for her office
I had let her down
I had let the whole school down

The driver dropped me off at my house
I went inside
   minister
   minister
   minister
pounded in my head
my mother was hanging clothes
in the sunny backyard
I went to the screen door, "Ma!"
"How did it go?: she asked

I burst into a torrent of words and tears
telling my sad tale
   the stupid mistake
   the cramps
   the angry principal
"You did your best, " my mother said
"Go upstairs. Get washed. Put on your play clothes.
Come help me hang these clothes."

I washed, changed, went into the yard
   minister
   minister
   minister
still pounding in my head

I picked up a wet shirt from the basket
pinned it to the clotheslinge
my mother smiled
we worked together
the humiliation fading
   clothespins
   sunshine
   my mother
all soothing balms
on that Saturday in May.

Bossa and Bossu

Bossa got lost on her way to the restroom

at my grandfather's wake

Comare Maria called her husband "Bossu"

Compare Gaetano called her "Bossa"

They were both the boss in their family

Bossa took a wrong turn on her way to the ladies room

at Leonetti's Funeral Parlor in South Philadelphia

she entered a room full of coffins

she was so shocked she could not move   could not scream

Bossu was among the many mourners

wife, children, grandchildren, siblings comari, compare, nieces,

nephews, cousins, godchildren, friends, neighbors,

gevella water customers

who packed the funeral home to honor my grandfather Pete

they told stories that he would have loved

Bossu with his son Joey was telling tales in Sicilian about

his and my grandfather's boyhood in San Pier Niceto, Sicilia

Joey asked his father where his mother was

he had not seen her in a while

Bossu knew she was gone too long   he went to search for her asked women coming out of the restroom if they had seen her

nobody had   he tried every door until he found his Bossa

frozen with fear among the coffins

"Bossu! Bossu!" she screamed when she saw him

"Bossa! Bossa!" he hollered grabbing her tightly

he pulled her out the door

rescued her from the coffins' thrall

Bossu and Bossa returned to the viewing

with another story to relate with drama and hilarity

Bossu and Bossa   Compare Gaetano and Comare Maria

that night honored my dear grandfather Pete

who dearly loved to tell

and dearly loved to hear

a good story.

A Visit

My nephew Julian has come down from New York to Philadelphia

    for a quick visit   a quick supper   a quick beer

    with his old aunts and uncles

he must board the bus back to Brooklyn at nine

we stand with him on a South Philly street corner

digging into our pockets

to fill his hands with cash for his journey

I see them right there with us

on that dark, wintry night

those shades of hard working men

those shades of hard working women

pulling out bills of fives, tens, twenties

with their rough hands

    as when years ago

    they put cash into our young hands for our journeys

We are a crowd of family under a street lamp

We are flesh, blood, and spirit

    necessity and love drive us all

    past   present   future

We carry on our pragmatic tradition.

Three Figs

Direct from the store on a hot July morning

you bound brilliant and sunny through the front door

in your hands

three green plump figs

wrapped in leaves

the first of the season

brought into the grocery from a neighbor's tree

It is still too soon for our backyard tree

to bear its large purple figs we will pick in September

You in the yellow Italian soccer shirt, I in the matching blue

delighted with the figs and each other

we laugh as though we still were the teenagers

we were when we first met

You say

as long as we are together

we will always be fifteen

It is high summer now in a light filled dining room

we savor and share three green figs on two china plates.

Once in a While

Once in a while
I allow myself to fantasize
about what it would be like
if you had lived
not died in your mid-thirties
but instead weathered the decades with me

   planting the garden

   playing with pets

   cooking pastina

   eating peaches

   crying over wars

   burying parents

mourning and exulting
cuddling through the withering and decaying
holding onto poetry, flowers, music

If you had made it with me
into old middle age
or middle aged old

   we could count each white hair on our heads

as a story of our lives entwined

each wrinkle a tale of heroism

each crease a sign of endurance

Yet you chose to die those many years ago

I still remain

you are strong in my memory

laughter, sadness, love combined

your hair always glossy black

your face ever young and righteous

Once in a while

I allow myself to fantasize

but I stop   I remember

I had you when I had you

No fantasies are necessary.

Diane Di Prima's Tangerine

In a Cleveland hotel room
Diane Di Prima
poet   innovator   pioneer
gave me a tangerine

In this gift of sweet fruit
"All I have to offer you is a tangerine, " she said
was her gentle graciousness
her hospitality
reaching back generations to Mediterranean lands

I took a tangerine from Diane Di Prima's hand
a strong hand that writes
nourishing poems   nurturing art

the tangerine our connection
to Sicily   and   Poetry
our citrus filled sensual mutual heritage

Diane Di Prima
American   Sicilian   Poet   Goddess
gave me a tangerine
gave me communion
gave me a blessing.

Pandemics

"Are you even afraid of the dead?"
Pietro Guaetta asked as he carried in his arms
the body of his sister Grazia
to the waiting undertaker and his wagon
the undertaker refused to enter the house
masked, he stood beside his horse
in a 1918 Pennsylvania coal mining town

Just a few years earlier
the teenagers, Pietro, long before he was my grandfather,
his sister Grazia, and brothers Nicola and Antonio
left their parents, left their sister Antonia and brother Francesco
left their stone house in sunny, disaster prone Sicily
for harsh Pennsylvania coalmines and company towns
lovely and exuberant Grazia cooked   cleaned
made their rented clapboard house a home
married fellow Sicilian miner Crispino Giacobello
Grazia and Crispino loved to laugh together
they had a baby daughter Natalina
Grazia was pregnant with her second that winter
when the Spanish Flu killed her and the unborn child

while flu-stricken Crispino hovered near death

these young Sicilians had survived earthquake   tidal wave

steerage   a world war   only to face

a global pandemic

when young and old sickened

when young and old died

fear prevailed   there was no cure

National Guardsmen surrounded the quarantined mining towns

No one permitted to enter or leave without a pass

"Are you even afraid of the dead?"

Pietro Guaetta   young   handsome   strong

sensitive   grieving   anguished

asked the undertaker as he loaded

his beloved sister's body into the cart

One hundred and two years later

Fear again grips the world

the coronavirus stalks old and young

family   friends   neighbors   sicken

famly   friends   neighbors   perish

images on TV of freezers loaded with corpses awaiting burial

I sit on my sofa in winter 2020

Isolated   in lockdown

grieving the deaths of loved ones

I sit alone   surrounded by

computer   television   phone   radio   books

online yoga   online work

online movies, meetings, opera, concerts

everything I need delivered to my door

I sit alone   I am in touch

I sit in luxury

compared to those immigrant siblings

who struggled a century ago

When Grazia died she left her baby daughter

in a house of men

her brother Pietro wrote a letter to

oldest brother Nicola

who lived with his young wife Idria and baby son

a few towns away

"Dear Brother, our dear sister Grazia has died

from influenza," Pietro wrote in Italian

in his beautiful ornate script

he learned to read and write in three years of school

in San Pier Niceto, Sicilia

"Will you come to take the baby Natalina to safety with your wife?

Our brother in-law Crispino is dying."

Sitting on my sofa, I think of them

new to this land of cold and snow

more than a century ago

they are now all gone   even Baby Natalina

who lived into her nineties

I think about Pietro's desperate question

"Are you even afraid of the dead?'

How would I answer it now

I know the language of this land

am educated   have many resources at hand

I am alone   I am in touch

"Are you even afraid of the dead?"

Nicola was not afraid

stoic   taciturn   he carried the baby blanket his wife gave him

walking at night through the cold back woods

slipping past armed National Guardsmen

with orders to shoot and kill anyone without a pass

Nicola arrived at the flu-ravaged house

took sleeping Natalina into his arms

wrapped her in the blanket

kept her safe and warm under his big overcoat

he tramped through the dark woods

eluded the Guard and their guns

traveling all night to his home where

Idria awaited with hot food and baby clothes

Idria cared for Natalina along with

her own baby son Giuseppe

raising them together

until a recovered Crispino came to claim his child

I am on the sofa   I ponder my grandfather's question

"Are you even afraid of the dead?"

When I am sad   I think of my Grandpop Pete

When I am scared   I think of my Uncle Nick

When I am confused I think of my Aunt Lizzie

Pietro   Nicola   Idria

All had taken American names

by the time I knew them

They had done what they needed to do

a century ago

with bravery   with a sense of what was right

I answer

I am not afraid of the dead

I know them   they inspire me

alone and in touch

I continue along with them.

Mindful

I recall

When I played in longest summer hours

and present lived in snowsuit and

first chilled sweater

Spring was just a now

and not a yearned for birth

Summer stilled and school was forever

Now, the children yet in school

I conjure mid-summer heat

to race and breathe a labor day

in the splendid morning sun

I feel the bed sway and sag,

sink, sing at midnight

Current shoes on paved streets

I'm sandaled on dusty, desert paths

I cook in sweltering July kitchen and

watch the blizzard rage

I listen to the radio

hear the orchestra

feel thirsty   taste peppermint

in a tiny room in Rome

On buses I'm on foot

on foot, I ride the waves

asleep I speak with the dead

kneeling by the corpse

we shop for bread and fruit

Back and forth I speed as

I glance at the eyes in the mirror.

PART TWO

THE SPARK OF SONGS

The Tragedy of Two Songs

When I was a toddler my mother used to sing to me

"Poor, Little Robin, walking, walking, walking to Missouri

he can't afford to fly

got a penny for Poor, Little Robin,

walking, walking, walking to Missouri

got a teardrop in his eye."

I loved this song, though it made me sad

I felt bad for Poor, Little Robin

When my mother pointed to the robins in the backyard

they all seemed fine

Why couldn't Poor, Little Robin fly?

Were his wings broken?

Did somebody hurt him?

Did he live in Philadelphia?

Was Missouri far away? Why did Poor, Little Robin have to go there?

Why was he poor? Do birds need money?

Could I send Poor, Little Robin money from my piggy bank?

For a while, my mother stopped singing the song because

I cried thinking about Poor, Little Robin

I begged her to sing the song again   I had to hear it

I sang along as I pictured Poor, Little Robin, along the highway

walking, walking, walking to Missouri

with a teardrop in his eye

My baby brother, Frankie, was born on July 3rd

on July 4th my mother sent me from her hospital lunch tray

a little red, white, and blue basket

filled with candy and a little American flag

my teenaged aunt brought it to me as I played

in my grandmother's backyard under the bedspread

thrown over the clothesline

to protect me from sun and heat

When Aunt Martha gave me the basket, she said,

"Mommy is thinking of you and will be home soon with Frankie"

Then, she began to sing

"A-tisket, A tasket, a brown and yellow basket"

I protested "My basket is red, white, and blue!"

I waved the flag as Aunt Martha sang,

"I sent a letter to my mommy

on the way, I dropped it

I dropped it, I dropped it, my little yellow basket"

I held my little basket tight

"A little girlie picked it up

and put it in her pocket

she took it, she took it

my little yellow basket

and if she doesn't bring it back

I think that I will die"

Oh, no! The basket got stolen by a mean girl!

I felt so bad for the little girl in the song

I imagined a mean girl stealing my basket

I needed to hold tight to my red, white, and blue basket

never drop it so it would not get stolen

Aunt Martha wanted me to sing along so I did

I sang along with this new tragedy

as bad as Poor, Little Robin's

"A-tisket, A-tasket

I lost my yellow basket

And if that girlie doesn't bring it back

I think that I will die."

I sang along with my mother and aunt

poverty, theft, meanness, heartache

all in these two tragic songs that I loved.

Coughing and Verdi

Pino and I went to see La Traviata

at the Opera House of Rome

we passed an old woman

in a heavy black coat

coughing

coughing

coughing

bent over   leaning against a wall

coughing

coughing

coughing

Pino whispered "poveraccia"

as we glanced at her before we entered

the glittering world of music and drama

Decades later,

in a heavy black coat

I go to see Il Trovatore

At Philadelphia's Academy of Music

coughing

coughing

coughing

bent over   leaning against a wall

I am a poveraccia now

coughing

coughing

coughing

Still,

sucking on three cough drops at once

I enter the glittering world of music and drama

Viva Verdi!

*poveraccia means *poor old thing*.

Nabucco

I cried for six hours straight

after seeing Verdi's Nabucco performed

by the Philadelphia Opera Company

Supernumerary Valentino

costumed as an Assyrian soldier

got me a ticket for the dress rehearsal

full orchestra   full production   full voices

the Academy of Music packed with

music teachers and music students

Italians first heard Nabucco in 1842

before they had a unified country

since the fall of Rome Italy partitioned dismissed

a geographical expression

that first Nabucco starred Giuseppina Strepponi

Giuseppe Verdi's majestic second wife

the opera's first Abigaille

when the chorus of Hebrew slaves yearning for their lost homeland

sang "Va Pensiero"

Italians heard their own longing for a united Italy

Verdi   the composer   the activist

Verdi   the artist   the patriot

was present at the birth of Italia, the country

twenty years of struggle   the Risorgimento

accompanied by Verdi's music

Here in the 21st century   here in Philadelphia   USA

"Va Pensiero" is played twice to satisfy

the audience's hunger to hear its beauty again

I begin to cry

It is Verdi's 200th birthday

At the finale

Teachers, students, and I clap, scream, cheer

stirred so deeply by Verdi's music and drama

I continue to cry

a giant Italian flag is lowered as a backdrop

the singers take their bows

I sob all the way down the aisle of the Academy of Music

I weep in the Ladies Room

I cry walking to the subway and on the train

I cannot stop

my sunglasses barely hide my swollen eyes

tears stream down even when I reach my home

O Peppino, the cells of your brain fired and opened
music poured forth as you wrote

O Maestro, you loved the land of your birth
Italia   in your head   heart   melodies

O Verdi, so much change over these two centuries
yet your music   your operas
touch the whole planet

I cry tears of joy and wonder.

Spring Bronchitis

Sparrows, kittens, squirrels, frogs

sing a fizzing chorus in my bronchial chords

sparrows, kittens, squirrels, frogs

sing a hissing chorus in my bronchial chords

tweets, mews, chirps, chirrups, and croaks

Spring   Spring   Spring

there are purple wildflowers in the garden

Spring   Spring   Spring

there are yellow wildflowers in the garden

Spring   Spring   Spring

there are tiny red rosebuds in the garden

sparrows, kittens, squirrels, and frogs in my throat

a choir chants in my chest

tweets, mews, chirps, chirrups, and croaks

Spring   Spring   Spring

there are tulips

there are hyacinths

sparrows, kittens, squirrels, frogs

happy for sunshine

happy for warmth

happy for breezes

tweets, mews, chirps, chirrups, and croaks

Spring   Spring   Spring

happy to breathe in Spring, Spring, Spring.

Visitation

I sleep warily on a snowy February night

with a stent in place around a kidney stone

at 2:01am I hear loud talking, music, static

I rise, look out the bedroom window

watch the snow fall silent and heavy

I walk downstairs   hear static, music, muffled voices

coming out of my turned off radio

I turn the knob on, then off again

pull the plug out of the socket

make sure there are no batteries in the radio

for twenty minutes I stand by the radio

static, music, muffled voices

my cat watches unalarmed

static, music, muffled voices

it may be a visitation from beyond

maybe my parents?

Mommy, Daddy, are you here?

Maybe Anita?

Anita, is it you?

Do they visit me in my distress?

I ask aloud for their help

grateful for their presence

I go back upstairs to bed and sleep

grateful for their presence

Static, music, and muffled voices continue.

The Father

When my grandfather Pietro Guaetta was a young man

he visited his mother's cousin, Mattia

was smitten by her eldest daughter

black haired   hazel eyed   seventeen year old Domenica

my future grandmother

In the 1920s, Pietro felt himself a modern man

after a few visits he wanted to know

if Domenica would have him before he asked

her father for her hand

During a passing moment while visiting

Pietro whispered to Domenica asking if she wanted him as her husband

If she did not, he would not foist himself upon her

Domenica whispered, "Ask my father. I want you as my husband.

That same day, after Pietro left, Domenica confided to her mother

what Pietro had asked   Mattia was delighted

That night, in her happiness, Mattia told her volatile husband

Pietro Bongiovanni about the young people

He flew into a rage over the insult

He ranted that he was the father

How dare this young man not ask him first for his daughter

He clutched his throat   lost his voice

took to his bed   refused to eat

After three days, Mattia sought out young Pietro

asked him to please go to her husband

apologize   make peace

otherwise, he would never marry beautiful Domenica

When young Pietro climbed the steps to the bedroom

Mattia and Domenica held their breath

Domenica's father sat silent in the bed

Pietro Guaetta apologized   he would have asked him for
    Domenica's hand

once he knew she wanted him, too

Pietro Bongiovanni fixed his bright blue eyes on

Pietro Guaetta's warm, brown eyes

he thundered, "How do you make the Sign of the Cross?"

young Pietro crossed himself, "In the Name of the Father…"

Domenica's father pounced

"The Father!   The Father!   The Father!

You start with the Father!

I am the Father!"

"You are the Father," said my grandfather Pietro Guaetta

"May I marry your daughter Domenica?"

"Yes. I am the Father and I say yes."

Domenica married Pietro because her father said yes.

Composer in the House

Between two and three each night

I wake to Dolly the cat's singing

Dolly the cat is an opera singer

trilling and rilling a cat cadenza

up and down the scales in feline bel canto

Dolly the cat is a composer

building melodies   reckless   loud   soft   plaintive

call and response   asking   answering

Maybe Dolly the cat sings and composes

to serenade the world at that hour

Maybe she is moved to compose and sing odes

to our quiet house, her toys, her food and water

Dolly the cat, singer and composer

wakes me to life's wonders.

Rich Girl Red Ghazal

Needing a new lipstick, this poor girl bought Rich Girl Red

she tried it on and learned it wasn't what the label said

Rich Girl Red was pale, sickly pink, and not at all red

she felt duped by the label's words, she had been misled

maybe rich girls are so in the black they never dread

having dull, faded lips; they have no need for red

the rich girls have lots of cash for their daily bread

while this poor girl's finances are always in the red

this poor girl may lack money but manages to be well fed

her politics are Green, she leads and is rarely led

certain that her lips must be prime, she now buys Certainly Red

she has known a little fame but never will use Rich Girl Red.

An Evening Out

At the dinner party

the guests talked of numbers in dreams

stock market schemes

powerball lottery wins

betting on horses, boxers, and cars

drinking African aperitifs and Portuguese wine

they toasted high stakes and liquidity

sipping soup   nibbling crepes

they longed for mystic tips on

how to get rich quick

munching fortune cookies

they searched the tea leaves in their cups

cast horoscopes of stars

gambled at cards

shot pool

rolled dice

Then, they all kissed goodnight

Promising tomorrow

they'd meet at the track.

Wilfred

Green-eyed son of Africa

you cannot know the comfort your words

have worked upon me through the years

since we sat together in History class

scholarly, we spoke of science and the arts

I'd then first beheld Benin bronzes

you, exquisite, pronounced them, yes, exquisite

Green-eyed son of Africa,

you worked with equations and chemicals

you told me life is one true song

I, island blooded, felt restless in duty's realm

so you gave me a balm:

Do what must be done in one sweet song

not caring as much for the written notes

as much as how the melody is sung.

PART THREE

THE FUSION OF
TERRITORIES

The Laurel

(inspired by Bernini's sculpture Apollo and Daphne at
the Galleria Borghese, Rome)

I don't know what I miss more

the running or the singing

Yet, I delight in the birds choosing me as their singing perch

I welcome the breezes that rustle my hair

Yes, I still think of all these leaves as my hair

though now it is evergreen and much more fragrant

than when it streamed black and long against the wind

as I ran blissful and free before he came

I have so many more limbs now than I once did

all reaching to heaven as when I raised my arms

to call upon Peneus, god of the river, my own father,

who heard my plea

I should be grateful, I suppose, for his rescue

I remember how he'd ask from his bed of waters

"Am I never to have a grandson?"

I, running off to deep woods,

singing a hymn to Diana, answered

"Father, let me be like Diana

I have made my vow

I want only freedom"

I never wanted lovers, earthly or divine,

Yet, the sun-lit god came to me one day

as I sang in these same grasses

He was beautiful and arrogant,

so like these athletes who now wear my hair

and lean against me and preen,

I tried to explain my vow

but he grew larger and fiery

he forced himself upon me

angry that I could spurn the god of poetry

I fought and ran swifter than ever toward the river

Apollo gained on me

I felt his hot breath upon my neck

he was a fingertip away

my arms upraised I cried

"Father, help me!"

At once I could not move

my legs took root and turned to wood

green shoots bloomed from my hands

my hair lifted itself to sprout these sturdy leaves

Ah, how the god of music screamed

as he touched my breast

and felt hard, brown bark

I was stunned, but still alive

my vow, my chastity, intact

Apollo caressed my trunk, bright tears filled his eyes

he mourned, "I love you and you are lost to me forever"

then, his body gleamed red and gold, as he plucked my hair

with my leaves in his hands he declared,

"You are my tree, my laurel,

my heroes, my victors, my poets

shall wreathe their brows with you

you are still my triumph"

He smiled and was gone and I've never seen him since

I may be his triumph but I was not defeated

though I lost my name and am

no longer Daphne of the woods

I am still beloved by Diana

She taught me much over the years

I see without eyes and hear without ears

I hear distant storms and the steps of ants

I know the intention of the hound

and scan the moods of the human heart

I have won my honor among the trees,

the learned, and the wise

Apollo fades and I endure

I am grateful for the gifts of the goddess

I am proud of the homage of men

Still,

I don't know what I miss more

the running or the singing

Fig Tree in the Yard

The Fig's chafed hands have spread over centuries

to shade, to feed

Mediterranean lands.

We smuggled her in our ramshackle ships

into this land of forests and rain.

We planted our precious mother tree

on tiny plots in small back yards

and still sit beneath her many hands

and seek a clue

to how she bound us to her bark

in ancient rites.

The questions of our displaced blood

She answers only with raised green veins,

Her tender fruit tastes

of sun-bathed lands and the fiber of the womb.

She bleeds in our pale hands

as we suck the juice

of burning earth and turquoise sea

and fused become again

with distant territory.

Eating Ossi di Morti on November 2

All Souls Day   far from Sicily
we watched Sicilian children on RAI TV News
clutch little plastic bags of ossi di morti
as they hold their parents' hands on the way to cemeteries
Today   here in Philadelphia   here in the USA
we buy our ossi di morti at the bakery
white hard cookies   bones of the dead
made of almond paste, flour, sugar, lemon juice, and cloves
in the shape of femurs, ulnas, and skulls
   we dunk them in espresso
   we dunk them in wine
   we dunk them in tea
   remember our dear departed
Nonna told us to pray for and to our dead always
they were looking out for us
Nonna told us if we prayed for and to our dead on November 1
the next morning they would bring ossi di morti
  and maybe a little money, too
Nonna said when she was a child in Sicily
her dear dead never failed to bring her
a bone cookie and a coin on November 2
even when they hardly had enough to eat
We dunk our ossi di morti to soften the hardness of our lives
  with the memories of our dead.

My Everyday Espresso

I put my little Bialetti espresso pot on the stove:

filtered water

arabica beans

ground up in the old way by

the Ginevra Family of Caltanisetta, Sicilia

I make this pot of coffee

not to drink but to smell

I stand by the stove

devouring the fragrance

that energizes and delights

When I was young

I brewed pots and pots of espresso

day and night   I drank cup after cup

while writing

while thinking

Giuseppe Verdi composed his music sipping espresso

calling it a balm for body and soul

Now, with ulcers and insomnia

I can no longer drink

sicilian, brazilian, american, hawaiian

or any kind of coffee

without discomfort

On Christmas, Easter, my birthday, and the Fourth of July

I drink a tiny cup of espresso

four times a year I feel the buzz

then the pain

knowing it was worth it

Today is just an everyday

nothing to celebrate

except for the scent of espresso, itself,

I inhale the intoxicating aroma

savor the espresso filled air

without taking even one sip

I let the pot sit on the stove for hours

at sunset I pour the liquid and grounds into the garden

Today, my lips and tongue might still long for espresso

Yet, my nose has been to heaven.

The Necropolis at Tarquinia

In the sea sunned afternoon

under the expanse of green

youth in sturdy boots

entered the tombs

hoisting electric spotlights

they caught glimpses of ancient days

where musicians played as maidens danced

animal leapt   athletes raced

all in vivid colors on the walls

the dead long gone from this place

only the paintings remain

the young people laughed   shouted

they speculated about the world

under this green expanse

What tune was played on flute as

the dancers stepped?

Did someone wail a dirge

at these seaside tombs?

How many wept?

The youth in sturdy boots

Snapped photos   wrote in notebooks

dimmed the artificial light

climbed the stone stairway to meet the sun..

To the Original People (Lenni Lenape of Eastern Pennsylvania)

Lenni Lenape,

your paths are the tarred and pavemented earth

       where once you walked moccasined and

       cared for the groves of tall pines

When you gazed at the blue, sweet-watered river

How could you know

those ships of men flesh and blood like you

would change the very texture of your green and purple land

They,

  with banners flying and swords cutting the sun's rays

  changed your very name to one of theirs

Delaware,

  I am with Europe's blood in me

  yet I would have liked to see

  a river shining below the towering pines

  and live amid those who walked moccasined

  and did not cut seedlings to pour hot tar

  on an earthen breast

Lenni Lenape,

  I'm not one of you renamed

  but I, too, am flesh and bone, displaced.

Winter Mood

The snow fell like manna as we lay sleeping

  hidden, afraid, leaden in concrete dreams

  of mask time of roaming virus

In the first morning hours

  the snow lay quietly in our paths

  sleeping, unafraid

Open to the lightest touch   the heaviest tread

Ready to be swept, blown, shoveled, vaporized...

The Possum

My neighbor trapped the possum in his yard

carries him out in a cage to his car for release in

FDR Park where other possums and wildlife live

among the trees and man-made lakes

I peer through the wires

catch the possum's frightened eyes

was this the possum I saw last night

at midnight in my yard taking a few bites of tender basil leaves

he held in his paws, his long hairless tail pointed straight up

his close set eyes above his snout looking straight at me

as I stared out the kitchen window

I look up possums on the internet

learn they are gentle solitary marsupials

who rather play dead than fight

I think of possums traveling Philly's streets in search of

people food in our trash cans

herbs, plants, and flowers in our gardens

I look into the possum's eyes

understand the possum, like me,

wants to survive happy and free.

What It Is

Pepper the therapy dog licks my hand

She seems to know my heart

Is it my bright, red shirt?

Is it my deep stare into her dark eyes?

Two month old Baby James smiles at me

A baby I don't know is delighted to see me

laughs   coos   pumps his fists   kicks his legs

as I pass his stroller and wave

Is it my fashionable Phillies baseball cap?

Is it my nearsighted squint behind sunglasses?

I wake to find a squirrel sitting on a table in my bedroom

the cat is fast asleep downstairs

I clap my hands   the squirrel jumps out the window

I throw pizzelle into the street for her to nibble

Is it my forest green nightshirt?

Is it my sleepy, bleary gaze?

One snowy winter, rats camp in my backyard garden

when I toss bread for birds and squirrels

the rats stay through the spring sunning themselves

I spray cayenne pepper and peppermint oil

The rats finally leave

Is it my blue sweatshirt?

Is it my startled gaze out of steamy windows?

I see our world through myopic, itchy eyes

yet I know we fellow creatures

are all on a journey together.

Pizzelle is a type of Italian waffle cookies

Two Murders

I witnessed two murders today

  within hours of each other

The cat caught and chewed the heads off two mice

I praised the cat for her hunting prowess

I pitied the mice who should not have entered

a home with a resident feline

Surely those mice smelled a cat

still they were compelled to risk death

  for shelter from the cold

  for tiny morsels of food

I petted the cat   gave her treats

wrapped the corpses in paper towels

said a prayer for their souls

set them in the trash because

there was too much ice in the garden

for a proper burial.

Nine Haiku

Possum at midnight
stares at me from the garden
we are both afraid.

It is too early
Dolly, the cat, wakes me up
even before dawn.

The last basil stalk
I pick shivering seeds
to store for summer.

Tall friend up ahead
cane in hand, I can't catch up
cold, hard rain pours down.

Sounds on a small stage
thrilling opera voices
on a windy night.

The cat's eyes accuse
I have come home very late
letting in the wind.

Hail pounds the windows
Nor'easter drops heavy snow
The old fence falls down.

Easter is early
icy howling winds wake us
snow on waving palms.

Blue wildflowers bloom
amid white patches of snow
Spring's promise in March.

Work

I head to work
leave Dolly my caped tabby cat at home
lounging on the sofa
food and water at the ready
Dolly has lined up my shoes upstairs
outside my bedroom door
later she'll bring them downstairs
to make designs and constructions
and sing to them
while I'm away
A block from the high rise where I work
I pass a bearded young beggar
sitting under a tree
an orange cat
a leash around his neck
sits upright and poised on the beggar's lap
no food or water in sight
the cat attracts attention and money
I cross busy Market Street to my job
I tutor   I teach
food and water in my backpack
cat or human
we work at tasks heavy or light
we all do what we must.

Cosmo House of Style

An elegant man in suit and tie

a small red feather in his stylish hat

stands on a city corner in polished shoes

handing out flyers

with sad, wary eyes

he is so careful

as he gives a sheet of paper

to each approaching man or woman

I extend my nail bitten fingers

to take the flyer from his manicured hand

I say, "Thank you"

"You are welcome," he says with an accent and hurt eyes

I read the flyer   Cosmo House of Style

Manicures and Pedicures: Discounts for Men and Women

I imagine walking into Cosmo House of Style

in my old coat and beat up sneakers

would everyone there be as elegant

as this dignified man on the corner?

If I asked for a manicure and pedicure

would they scoff at my arthritic hands and calloused heels?

The flyer lists the prices for Cosmo House of Style

They are beyond my budget even with the discount

so I walk past the elegant man

wondering if he's the owner of Cosmo House of Style

or just somebody once a professional   once a businessman

who needs a job in a new land

and does that job as well as he can

handing out flyers for Cosmo House of Style

with honor and with care.

Baby, Baby Shark

Billions of neurons

Baby, Baby Shark

Yards of intestine

Baby, Baby Shark

Blood   Heart   Lungs

Baby, Baby Shark

Electrical Impulses

Feeling skin   Breathing skin   Shark skin

Baby, Baby Shark

Powerful cells alive and driving

Dream in a predator brain

Baby, Baby Shark

Swimming through sun tipped waters

Swimming through gold and red tinged waters

Slipping through high and low blue waves

The ocean depth   the sand   the air   the prey

Baby, Baby Shark

Learning   Cruising   Hunting

Baby, Baby Shark.

Corn Maiden Kachina

I brought home from Hopi Land

a hand carved Corn Maiden Kachina

one foot tall

she holds a dish of corn in

  her outstretched right hand

  her left hand fisted at her side

Corn Maiden Kachina wears

traditional Hopi ceremonial garb

  black trimmed white dress and boots

  her stylized kachina face

  below a blue-feathered red-ribbonned head dress

I chose Corn Maiden Kachina

among the many kachinas of Hopi artists

because she spoke to me of power

                  of bravery

                  of nurturance

When I brought Corn Maiden Kachina

from Arizona to my Philadelphia home

I placed her atop a bookcase

near my grandmother's bronze

1939 New York World's Fair Statue of Liberty souvenir

Now, many years later,

I look at Corn Maiden Kachina

realize she has done her job

                of inspiration

                of calling down protection and

                sustenance

she stands so close to that other symbol of inspiration

which welcomed my family from their Old World home

into the New World which ever remains Corn Maiden Kachina's
Old World

From their bookcase perch

the Lady with the dish of corn

the Lady with the torch

stare down at me

Corn Maiden Kachina and the Statue of Liberty

Their worlds collide

 coincide

co-exist in me.

Acknowledgments

Grateful acknowledgment is made to the editors of the following publications where some of the poems in this book first appeared:

21 Poems; First Wave: Beach Bards Anthology; Dante Review of Canberra; Modern Haiku; Moonstone Poetry Ink Anthology; Ovunque Siamo; Paterson Literary Review; Penn Laurel Poets; Philadelphia Poets; Row Home Magazine; and Unbearables.

The following poems have been awarded as follows:

"A Visit," Editor's Choice, Allen Ginsberg Poetry Awards, 2022

"Trigger," Honorable Mention, Allen Ginsberg Poetry Awards, 2021

"Daddy's Little Cap," Honorable Mention, Allen Ginsberg Poetry Awards, 2020

"Easting Ossi di Morti on November 2," Honorable Mention, Allen Ginsberg Poetry Awards, 2019

About the Author

MARIA FAMÀ is the author of eight books of poetry. Her work appears in numerous publications and has been anthologized. Famà has read her poetry in many cities across the United States, read one of her short stories on National Public Radio, and recorded her poetry for CD compilations of music and poetry. Maria Famà did her undergraduate and graduate work in History at Temple University. She appears in the film documentaries, "Prisoners Among Us," "Pipes of Peace," and "La Mia Strada: My Way," reading her poems. She was awarded the Aniello Lauri Award for Creative Writing in 2003 and 2005. In 2008, she was awarded the Amy Tritsch Needle Award for Poetry. In 2018, Famà won second prize in the Allen Ginsberg Poetry Awards. In 2019, she received the Petracca Award for her poetry. Her latest books are: *The Good for the Good*, published by Bordighera Press in 2019; *Other Nations: an animal journal*, published by Pearlsong Press in 2017; and *Mystics in the Family*, published in 2013 by Bordighera Press. Maria Famà lives and works in Philadelphia.

VIA FOLIOS

A refereed book series dedicated to the culture of Italians and Italian Americans.

DANIELA GIOSEFFI. *Blood Autumn/Autunno di sangue*. Vol 39. Poetry.
FRED MISURELLA. *Lies to Live By*. Vol 38. Stories.
STEVEN BELLUSCIO. *Constructing a Bibliography*. Vol 37. Italian Americana.
ANTHONY JULIAN TAMBURRI, Ed. *Italian Cultural Studies 2002*.
    Vol 36. Essays.
BEA TUSIANI. *con amore*. Vol 35. Memoir.
FLAVIA BRIZIO-SKOV, Ed. *Reconstructing Societies in the Aftermath of War*.
    Vol 34. History.
TAMBURRI. et al., Eds. *Italian Cultural Studies 2001*. Vol 33. Essays.
ELIZABETH G. MESSINA, Ed. *In Our Own Voices*.
    Vol 32. Italian/American Studies.
STANISLAO G. PUGLIESE. *Desperate Inscriptions*. Vol 31. History.
HOSTERT & TAMBURRI, Eds. *Screening Ethnicity*.
    Vol 30. Italian/American Culture.
G. PARATI & B. LAWTON, Eds. *Italian Cultural Studies*. Vol 29. Essays.
HELEN BAROLINI. *More Italian Hours*. Vol 28. Fiction.
FRANCO NASI, Ed. *Intorno alla Via Emilia*. Vol 27. Culture.
ARTHUR L. CLEMENTS. *The Book of Madness & Love*. Vol 26. Poetry.
JOHN CASEY, et al. *Imagining Humanity*. Vol 25. Interdisciplinary Studies.
ROBERT LIMA. *Sardinia/Sardegna*. Vol 24. Poetry.
DANIELA GIOSEFFI. *Going On*. Vol 23. Poetry.
ROSS TALARICO. *The Journey Home*. Vol 22. Poetry.
EMANUEL DI PASQUALE. *The Silver Lake Love Poems*. Vol 21. Poetry.
JOSEPH TUSIANI. *Ethnicity*. Vol 20. Poetry.
JENNIFER LAGIER. *Second Class Citizen*. Vol 19. Poetry.
FELIX STEFANILE. *The Country of Absence*. Vol 18. Poetry.
PHILIP CANNISTRARO. *Blackshirts*. Vol 17. History.
LUIGI RUSTICHELLI, Ed. *Seminario sul racconto*. Vol 16. Narrative.
LEWIS TURCO. *Shaking the Family Tree*. Vol 15. Memoirs.
LUIGI RUSTICHELLI, Ed. *Seminario sulla drammaturgia*.
    Vol 14. Theater/Essays.
FRED GARDAPHÈ. *Moustache Pete is Dead! Long Live Moustache Pete!*.
    Vol 13. Oral Literature.
JONE GAILLARD CORSI. *Il libretto d'autore. 1860 - 1930*. Vol 12. Criticism.
HELEN BAROLINI. *Chiaroscuro: Essays of Identity*. Vol 11. Essays.
PICARAZZI & FEINSTEIN, Eds. *An African Harlequin in Milan*.
    Vol 10. Theater/Essays.
JOSEPH RICAPITO. *Florentine Streets & Other Poems*. Vol 9. Poetry.
FRED MISURELLA. *Short Time*. Vol 8. Novella.
NED CONDINI. *Quartettsatz*. Vol 7. Poetry.
ANTHONY JULIAN TAMBURRI, Ed. *Fuori: Essays by Italian/American
    Lesbiansand Gays*. Vol 6. Essays.
ANTONIO GRAMSCI. P. Verdicchio. Trans. & Intro. *The Southern Question*.
    Vol 5. Social Criticism.
DANIELA GIOSEFFI. *Word Wounds & Water Flowers*. Vol 4. Poetry. $8

WILEY FEINSTEIN. *Humility's Deceit: Calvino Reading Ariosto Reading Calvino.*
  Vol 3. Criticism.
PAOLO A. GIORDANO, Ed. *Joseph Tusiani: Poet. Translator. Humanist.*
  Vol 2. Criticism.
ROBERT VISCUSI. *Oration Upon the Most Recent Death of Christopher Columbus.*
  Vol 1. Poetry.

www.ingramcontent.com/pod-product-compliance
Lightning Source LLC
Chambersburg PA
CBHW020207090426
42734CB00008B/968